THE MISSING ENTRIES
WORDS FOR SURVIVAL

NAJYA WILLIAMS

NAJYA WILLIAMS

THE MISSING ENTRIES

COPYRIGHT © 2023 NAJYA A. WILLIAMS
ALL RIGHTS RESERVED

All rights are reserved. The book and all subcomponents of the book may not be reproduced, duplicated or utilized in any shape, form or fashion with the exception of short passages used in literary reviews. Any use must be approved by the author of this book, Najya A. Williams.

The front cover of this book was designed and illustrated by Kavita Sundaram, and is copyright © protected. Any use of the image outside of what is permitted by the illustrator, author and publisher is strictly prohibited.

Digitally distributed in the United States of America

The BGM Press
najyawilliams.com

THE MISSING ENTRIES
WORDS FOR SURVIVAL

NAJYA WILLIAMS

THE MISSING ENTRIES

for
Amari-Grey
linguist, creative, divine

NAJYA WILLIAMS

Hi beautiful human,

First and foremost, thank you for taking the time to explore this offering – I remain awed by and grateful for your support of my art.

A lot has happened since I released my debut chapbook, *Cotton*, in 2017. I produced and released my own spoken word album, *mad black woman*, in 2019. I graduated from Harvard, earning my A.B in Sociology with high honors. I am an M.D. and Narrative Medicine graduate certificate candidate at the Lewis Katz School of Medicine. I've spent time in silent and communal reflection via several retreats and residencies, including Obsidian, Sundress, Southern Esesu Endeavor and Rutgers Poets and Scholars. It's been a beautifully generative time and I can't properly express my gratitude for the ways God and my spirit guides have held me so tenderly through these experiences.

Now, I am gearing up for my first full-length poetry book, to be published by one of the largest entities in the industry, and I feel it's only right that I offer a special gift to my community while we wait. *The Missing Entries: Words for Survival* is a microchapbook that reimagines the pocket dictionary as we know it. *What happens when we write our own definitions? What do we learn from the quiet space beneath*

THE MISSING ENTRIES

the surface of words? What threads emerge when we place them in conversation with each other?

This project was inspired by a writing exercise offered by Raymond Antrobus, one of my Obsidian Retreat tutors who I had the pleasure of learning from. I hope to have done the craft he has sown into me and my peers justice.

It is my hope that this project lifts, challenges, and inspires you in the most unimaginable way. Cheers and the happiest of reading to you!

love and light,
N

NAJYA WILLIAMS

THE MISSING ENTRIES

Amend (v.)
    to disturb the status quo

origin: the Age of Revolution (1760-present)

If our goal in life is not to *amend* the very soil of all the land we set foot on, what are we doing?

Audience (n.)
    an image of bones

origin: the stars across the Milky Way galaxy

As I formed in my mother's womb, her ribs became my first *audience.*

Basket (n.)
    keeper of the truth

origin: the vocal cords of West African griots

When my grandchildren search for ancient wisdom, I will be the *basket* they can start with.

Belong (v.)
    to hold close to the bosom

origin: the space between a child and parent in a baby-wearing sling

One can only feel safe enough to grow if they feel safe enough to *belong*.

THE MISSING ENTRIES

Church (n.)
    where the shit turns into sustenance

origin: under the lap cloths of the elders

I never leave *church* the same way I first came in.

Currency (n.)
    an object to capture memories

origin: the transatlantic slave trade

My ancestors and I understand a different *currency*, but know identical prices.

Dinner (n.)
    give and take in practice

origin: the period after a day of rest

He was invited over for Sunday *dinner*, and left with a belly and spirit full.

Dirt (n.)
    gathering place for the gossips and good-doers

origin: pangea

If we getting it out the mud, does that mean we gotta stay in the *dirt*?

THE MISSING ENTRIES

Enjambed (adj.)
    an illusion of impermeability

origin: fence straddling

They thought there was safety in being *enjambed* between their values and lived reality.

Error (n.)
    a slice of stress

origin: the Garden of Eden

Every *error* leaves a bitter wound on my spirit – it is why I am afraid to make them.

Failure (n.)
    a learning opportunity

origin: the elementary school gradebook

With every *failure*, I rewrite my brain to hold more knowledge.

Fly (v.)
    to journey curiously

origin: the first pair of birds created

Every day of your life is an opportunity to *fly* – if only you believe that you are free to do so.

THE MISSING ENTRIES

Glance (v.)
    to engage silently

origin: the eyes of a Black mama

She *glanced* at her friend, and a whole conversation floated in the air.

Guest (n.)
    a holder of unusual things

origin: the fence between home and neighbor

The bride was afraid she did not have enough food for every *guest*, but was later stunned by the overflow that was produced.

Heartsease (n.)
    red chested beauty

origin: the quilt sewn by my grandmother

She is more than a *heartsease* – she is the beat between beats.

Historian (n.)
    an uncompromising spine

origin: the autobiographies of my ancestors

As the world rushes to fictionalize reality, my community will rest upon the strength of the *historian*.

THE MISSING ENTRIES

Insect (n.)
    a bee's redemption arc

origin: the honeycombs

To understand the frequency of an *insect* is to know that it would rather sweeten than sting.

Investment (n.)
    the foundation for success

origin: the sacrifice of community; mutual aid

One cannot build a longstanding home without pouring an *investment* into its raw frame.

Jostle (v.)
    to intentionally sweeten

origin: the shifting of tectonic plates

He *jostled* the love we share when he saw me without being asked to.

Judgment (n.)
1) a come to Jesus meeting/ invitation
2) A form of apology or olive branch

origin: the melody of tears

When I was invited to *judgment*, my heart became open to honest self-reflection.

THE MISSING ENTRIES

Keep (v.)
     to find home within

origin: the sowing of creole and Gullah culture into plantation grounds

The common thread that ties together all of my chosen family is that they are simply easy to *keep*.

Kite (n.)
     to make gravity bend to your will

origin: Ancient Chinese dreamers

When I open my mouth, I allow my words to shapeshift into a *kite* until the stars rest beneath my feet.

Lake (n.)
    a new addition to the ecosystem

origin: healing circles

A *lake* moved into town — God answered our prayers with more than five loaves of bread and two fish.

Listen (v.)
    to have insatiable thirst

origin: the call-and-response of field hollers and Negro spirituals

synonym: reason

To truly *listen* requires more from our bodies than just the attention of our ears.

THE MISSING ENTRIES

Market (n.)
    The future and present and conversation with each other

origin: prehistoric barter systems

At the *market*, we trade our trauma for collective liberation and generational healing.

Morsel (n.)
    a detail of a person

origin: the crumbs leftover at the end of a long shift

It took a long time for me to grow comfortable with holding all the *morsels* of myself.

Negotiation (n.)
    the space between a rock and a hard place

origin: the lesser of two evils

There is no *negotiation* that will soothe hunger or save housing when the account is already overdrawn.

Non-assimilating (adj.)
    to be weapon and balm

origin: the kinks of 4c hair

Black people understand the power and responsibility it is to be *non-assimilating*.

THE MISSING ENTRIES

Oak (n.)
    a living, breathing body

origin: the roots of ancestral family trees

She is a small *oak* in this community, but that truth is all we needed to be life devoted conservationists.

Offend (v.)
    to traverse life

origin: the footprints left in wet concrete

I believe that it is my duty and obligation to *offend*, as fully and wholly as possible.

NAJYA WILLIAMS

Panel (n.)
    a spread of nice things

origin: my grandmother's china closet

This love-filled home is part of a larger *panel* that makes life all the easier to exist within.

Partner (v.)
To work ~~hand~~ heart in ~~hand~~ heart

origin: the first play date between small children

My friend and I *partnered* with each other because our souls had already become inextricably linked.

THE MISSING ENTRIES

Quality (n.)
      just a smidge of a being

origin: Eve's curiosity

For every *quality* I allow you to see, there are a thousand more hidden beneath my skin.

Quiet (n.)
      the fragrance of peace

origin: the scent of my mother's arms

Most days, I like to bathe in the *quiet*, but sometimes, it becomes a bit too unsettling.

Reason (v.)
    to have insatiable thirst

origin: the djembe drum beating under a rib cage

synonym: listen

I spent my life *reasoning* for all that I could understand — my cup is finally full.

Road (n.)
    a tethering

origin: the space between start and end

We never truly meet the end of the *road* — there is always more pulling us ahead.

Strength (n.)
      bodily fluids (i.e. blood, sweat, tears)

origin: the proteins encoded by mitochondrial DNA

I never had to find my *strength* — it was always sustaining me even when I couldn't see it.

Swim (v.)
      to root in reality

origin: the plunge into the deep end

She *swam* tentatively at first, but with some lessons, became an all-star athlete who cultivated resilience.

Tenant (n.)
    the ear beyond the mirror

origin: a black box theater production

He spoke to a *tenant* about his experience, but didn't realize they already met before.

Tradition (n.)
    an opinion devoid of grace

origin: the line between suggestion and demand

I can respect *tradition* and still reject it from the sanctity of my space.

THE MISSING ENTRIES

Union (n.)
	the absence of chaos

origin: the sky's junction with the surface of the earth

I watch the *union* of night and day from the shore, an overwhelming peace washing over me.

Us (n.)
	a group of brains

origin: twins in the womb

When society sees *us*, they know we have been tethered since the beginning of time.

Virus (n.)
    a resistance, proudly

origin: the loss of microorganisms during the rise of humanity

Our oppressor calls us wild, untamable savages but I prefer to be considered a *virus*, parasitic even.

Voice (v.)
    to intentionally leave a mark

origin: the hieroglyphics etched onto cavern walls

We *voiced* our dreams into the atmosphere until they became too great for the universe to ignore.

THE MISSING ENTRIES

Wander (v.)
>to offer quiet, scintillating gaze

origin: the mind of the introverted genius

The way she **wanders** unapologetically can feel threatening to the people around her.

Worry (n.)
>an intruder

origin: the single parent trying to make a dollar from fifteen cents

There is overwhelming evidence that proves how **worry** stole years from my mother's body — but this is not a case that will hold up in the court of law.

X-ray (n.)
    a winding path

origin: the stairway to Heaven

An *X-ray* is not easy to understand, but rewarding when you look at it in the context of the full picture.

Xylophone (n.)
    a human

origin: the hominins

We saw a group of *xylophones* making sounds in the park - some called it "laughter" and others called it "music".

THE MISSING ENTRIES

Yearn (v.)
    to befriend water

origin: the aquatic animals and microorganisms who have survived multiple iterations of this earth

They learned to *yearn* in gentle sprinkles, storms, blessing downpours, and hurricanes alike.

Youth (n.)
    a means to make music

origin: the crescendo and decrescendo of newly formed ocean waves

The *youth* are the instruments that will craft the sound of the revolution.

Zenaida (n.)
    an object to capture memories

origin: the amygdala, hippocampus, cerebellum and pre-frontal cortex of the brain

If children are *zenaidas*, why do we question the images they eventually develop and show us?

Zigzag (v.)
    to trace the curves of a conscience

origin: the first pursuit of self-identity, self-realization, and self-actualization

Life constantly *zigzags*, teaching us to be flexible enough to evolve but solid enough to remain standing.

THE MISSING ENTRIES

NAJYA WILLIAMS

THE MISSING ENTRIES

UBUNTU
"I am because we are."

First and foremost, this project would not have happened without the grace and guidance that my God, ancestors and spirit guides covered me with throughout this process - to them, I offer my most sincere gratitude.

To my mama and grandmama, the matriarchs of our family and the first warriors I've ever known – it is your resilience and tenacity that flowed through my veins and brought me to this place.

To Kavita, the creative visionary who was ready and willing to breathe life into the cover of this project – your "yes" is one that I will always cherish.

To my chosen family, thank you for always receiving my words with eager hearts, minds, and souls. You remain an answered prayer.

To my mentors, thank you for your unwavering faith in me and my talents. What a privilege it is to view myself through your kind eyes.

To my extended family, friends, and supporters, thank you for trusting me once again. It is your love that provides the wind beneath my wings.

To Raymond Antrobus and my Obsidian Foundation family, thank you for pushing my pen into new, exciting places. I am not who I once was because of you.

THE MISSING ENTRIES

YOUR TURN

Use the table below to write your own definitions to some of the words that were included in this collection. After you've written the definitions, mix and match the list of words and definitions.

Take a moment to reflect on what you unearth and discover. What emotions come up? What does your spirit call you to write further about? Where is your pen taking you?

Feel free to share what you create on Instagram and tag Najya (@NajyaWilliams) or via her website, najyawilliams.com

heartsease	
non-assimilating	
offend	
quiet	
wander	

THE MISSING ENTRIES

NAJYA WILLIAMS

THE MISSING ENTRIES

NAJYA WILLIAMS

MEET THE AUTHOR

Najya Williams (she/her) is a multidisciplinary artist who floats along the U.S. East Coast. Najya is an advocate for self-care and self-preservation, especially within the Black community, and this passion is reflected in many of her projects, service efforts and literary works. Her poetry, essays, and other writings have been accepted and/or published by a number of organizations, including *POETRY Magazine, Black Youth Project and Healing Points*. Currently, she is also a Managing Editor for the *Katz Journal of Medicine*, Poetry Reader for the *Chestnut Review*, and Board of Director Member for *Girls Health Ed*.

MEET THE ILLUSTRATOR

Kavita Megha (they/them) is a multimedia illustrator based in Central Illinois, originally from Massachusetts. Kavita revels in the experience of storytelling and witnessing the stories of others, and strives to always be seeking new information and perspective, no matter how uncomfortable. Their work arises from a desire to connect with others over these things. They are a first year tattoo artist and student pursuing a degree in Studio Art. When not drawing, they work at a home improvement store and are part of a local harm reduction supplies-share to support safe drug use for the public.

THE MISSING ENTRIES

NAJYA WILLIAMS

THE MISSING ENTRIES

www.ingramcontent.com/pod-product-compliance
Lightning Source LLC
Chambersburg PA
CBHW051712090426
42736CB00013B/2669